Outlaws and Lawmen of the Wild West

BILLY THE KID

Carl R. Green

➤ and ❖

William R. Sanford

ENSLOW PUBLISHERS, INC.

Bloy St. and Ramsey Ave.   P.O. Box 38
Box 777   Aldershot
Hillside, N.J. 07205   Hants GU12 6BP
U.S.A.   U.K.

Library of Congress Cataloging-in-Publication Data

Green, Carl R.
  Billy the Kid / Carl R. Green and William R. Sanford.
    p. cm. — (Outlaws and lawmen of the wild west)
  Includes bibliographical references and index.
  Summary: Traces the brief and violent life of the outlaw who
gained notoriety throughout the West.
  ISBN 0-89490-364-0
  1. Billy, the Kid—Juvenile literature. 2. Outlaws—Southwest,
New—Biography—Juvenile literature. 3. Frontier and pioneer life—
Southwest, New—Juvenile literature. [1. Billy the Kid.
2. Robbers and outlaws. 3. Southwest, New—History—1848-]
I. Sanford, William R. (William Reynolds), 1927- . II. Title.
III. Series: Green, Carl R. Outlaws and lawmen of the wild west.
F786.B54G74 1992
364.1′552′092—dc20
[B]   91-18124
                                                                CIP
                                                                 AC

Printed in the United States of America

10 9 8 7 6 5 4 3 2 1

Illustration Credits: Arkansas Department of Parks and Tourism, p. 30;
Carl R. Green and William R. Sanford, pp. 8, 18, 38; Museum of New Mexico,
pp. 6, 20, 35, 42; Robert N. Mullin Collection, N.S. Haley Memorial Library,
pp. 10, 16, 32, 36, 39; Special Collections, University of Arizona Library, pp.
17, 21, 23, 24, 25, 37, 43; Western History Collections, University of Oklahoma Library, pp. 12, 27, 40.

Cover Illustration: Bettmann Archive

CONTENTS

AUTHORS' NOTE

This book tells the true story of the outlaw Billy the Kid. The Kid was as well-known a hundred years ago as rock stars are now. People all over the country talked about the Kid. The newspapers of the day printed stories about his crimes. Thus, the stories and quotes used in this book come from firsthand reports.

1

THE KID'S FIRST ESCAPE

In 1875, Henry Antrim was fifteen years old. He was living in Silver City, New Mexico. His mother was dead, and he had been taken in by Mrs. Sarah Brown and her family. Henry was small for his age. No one guessed that one day he would be the well-known outlaw Billy the Kid.

Even then, Henry was no angel. He stole some butter and sold it to a Silver City store. The sheriff soon tracked down the thief. He thought he knew how to deal with the boy. Turning Henry over his knee, the sheriff gave him a spanking.

But Henry did not change. As he did all his life, he chose his friends poorly. One friend was a thief called Sombrero Jack. Jack took some clothes from a Chinese laundry and gave them to Henry to hide at the Brown house. When Mrs. Brown found the bundle she called the sheriff.

Sombrero Jack ran off, leaving Henry to take the blame. The sheriff punished the boy more strongly this time. He put Henry in jail.

Because he was so young, Henry was not put in a jail cell. He was given a bed in a hallway instead. If Henry had served his time he soon would have been set free. But he made one more bad choice. Henry waited until the sheriff went to lunch. Then he climbed up the chimney and escaped. Once he was out of jail, Henry fled from Silver City.

Four years passed before Henry Antrim became known as Billy the Kid. But his life as an outlaw had already begun.

Silver City, New Mexico was a frontier mining town in the 1870s. Henry Antrim had his first run-ins with the law while growing up here. The young thief later became better known as William Bonney— Billy the Kid.

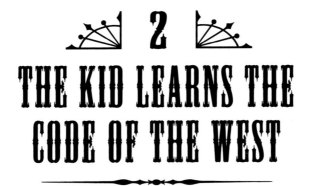

2

THE KID LEARNS THE CODE OF THE WEST

Western writers agree that Billy the Kid was born in New York City. The baby was given the name Henry by his mother, Catherine McCarty. Born in Ireland, Catherine came to America to escape a famine. Henry had a brother, Joe. Beyond these basics, the writers often differ in their stories.

When was Henry born? The records show he was most likely born on November 23, 1859. What happened to his father? He may have died when the boy was very young. Some say the man was murdered. Was Joe older or younger than Henry? No one knows.

Henry's life is easier to trace after Catherine moved west with her sons. In Minnesota she met William Antrim. The two fell in love, but did not marry right away. They soon moved to Wichita, Kansas. Catherine washed clothes for a living. She was a hard worker and her laundry

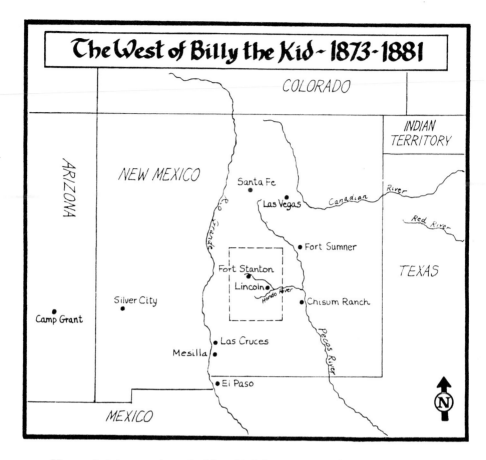

The West of Billy the Kid - 1873-1881

Henry Antrim was born in New York but grew up in New Mexico. It was here that he grew to manhood and found fame as the outlaw Billy the Kid. The area of the Lincoln County War (enclosed by dotted line) appears in greater detail on page 18.

business did well. But then she fell ill. A doctor examined her and said her lungs were diseased. There was only one treatment. She had to move to a high, dry climate.

Catherine and William took the boys to Santa Fe, New Mexico. The couple was married there in 1873. Next, the family's search for a good climate led them to Silver City, New Mexico. This mining town lies in the southwest corner of the state.

The Antrims lived in a log cabin near a stream. William worked at odd jobs when he was not looking for gold. Catherine took in boarders to help pay the bills. Young Henry watched his mother grow weaker and weaker. Soon the time came when she could not leave her bed. Catherine died in 1874.

Henry was still in school when his mother died. The small, thin boy was a good student. Now, with his mother dead, he lost interest in schoolwork. He also found it hard to get along with his stepfather. Henry solved the problem by quitting school and moving in with the Brown family. He paid for his keep by working in a butcher shop. In later years, the people of Silver City recalled Henry's love of music and dancing. He even took part in a show held at the opera house.

Growing up in Silver City left a mark on Henry. Life there was violent. The men carried guns, and many were quick to use them. Some gambled and drank too much. Henry began to believe that only fools work hard for money. It seemed easy to take what one wanted, no matter what the law said.

Henry also learned the "Code of the West." One of the rules was that all wrongs must be avenged. To do nothing in the face of an insult was the coward's way. When Henry escaped from the Silver City jail he was only fifteen. But he soon proved that he could take care of himself.

Henry went to Arizona after he left Silver City. He

found a job on a ranch near Camp Grant. A town boy all his life, Henry did not know how to be a cowboy. He had to learn how to ride a horse, rope a cow, and fire a gun. He learned quickly, but he was a boy trying to do a man's job. The ranch foreman soon fired him.

In 1876, Henry made another bad choice. He joined a gang of small-time thieves. Henry's best friend in the gang was John Mackie. Mackie, who was older, had been in trouble before. The two began by stealing saddles and blankets. Growing bolder, they began to steal horses. After each theft, they rode to far-off ranches and sold the stolen animals.

Henry soon stole a horse from the wrong man. Sergeant Lewis Hartman and four friends tracked Henry northward. They caught up with the thief near Globe City,

Henry Antrim watched cowboys, miners, and settlers ride down this dusty Silver City street. He made a bad choice of friends here. Older men taught him that it was easier to steal than to work for a living.

Arizona. Hartman took back his horse and left Henry on foot. A few months later, the sergeant filed a complaint. The sheriff put Henry in jail.

Henry did not like jails. He threw salt in a guard's eyes and tried to escape. Other guards caught him and locked iron chains to his legs. Henry escaped again that night, chains and all. In the weeks that followed he was caught twice more, escaping each time.

The trouble died down by the summer of 1877. Henry drifted back to Camp Grant. People now called him "Kid" because he looked so young. One thing about the Kid was not childlike. He wore a pistol stuffed under his belt.

The Kid was quick to laugh and most people liked him. But one man, Windy Cahill, went out of his way to tease him. The big blacksmith thought it was fun to slap the Kid and knock him down. One day the two called each other mean names. That started a real fight. As they wrestled, Cahill pinned the Kid to the floor. With his free hand, the Kid pulled out his pistol. The gun roared and Cahill fell over, shot in the stomach. The blacksmith died the next day.

A jury ruled that the shooting was murder. The Kid did not wait to be put in jail. He rode east to New Mexico and holed up on a ranch near Silver City. The people there did not ask questions. They fed their guest and gave him a bed. But the Kid thought the law was on his trail. Two weeks later he took to the road again.

The teenage ranch hand who became Billy the Kid poses for this portrait. Billy killed his first man not long after this photo was taken.

3
THE KID MOVES TO LINCOLN COUNTY

Henry "Kid" Antrim was growing up. When he left Silver City he was a small-time thief. Now, two years later, he was a horse thief and cattle rustler. He had killed his first man. When he had money, he went to saloons to dance and play cards. Unlike most of his friends, he did not smoke or drink.

At seventeen the Kid was a slim, wiry young man. He weighed 135 pounds and looked taller than his five feet eight inches. His hair was light brown, and his eyes were blue. When he smiled his two front teeth stuck out. The easy smile won him many sweethearts. Mexican girls also liked his blue eyes and good Spanish.

Some writers say the Kid dressed like a movie cowboy. They write about his "buckskin pants with gold bells sewed to the sides." His hat, they say, was covered with gold and jewels. The stories are not true. In fact, the

Kid dressed simply. He wore a dark coat and pants, a vest, and polished boots. His hat was a Mexican sombrero with a green band.

Even though he was an outlaw, the Kid was easy to like. He was generous, brave, and full of fun. Unlike many cowboys, he could read and write. When he was in a tight spot he often cracked a joke. But his good humor hid a fierce temper. When he was angry he acted without thinking. The Kid had a good mind, but he did not always use it. When it came to his friends, he was very loyal. This trait often led him into more trouble.

After leaving the ranch near Silver City, the Kid joined a gang of rustlers. Jesse Evans led the gang from its base at Mesilla, New Mexico. They stole horses and cattle in that state and in Texas. They even crossed the border into Mexico to steal cattle. Life with the Evans gang completed the Kid's training in the outlaw life. He became a crack shot with both pistol and rifle.

In September 1877, the gang stole three horses from a camp in the Burro Mountains. The owners were able to track the thieves. They came back to Mesilla to say that Kid Antrim was part of the gang. The news was printed in the local paper. Once again, the Kid and his friends were wanted by the law.

With the law after them, the gang broke up. The Kid still worried that he might be jailed for shooting Windy Cahill. Friends told him to hide in Mexico. But Jesse Evans led what was left of the gang to New Mexico's

Lincoln County. The county was a hard three-day ride away. It seemed far enough from Arizona to be safe. The Kid could not have known he was heading into a war when he decided to rejoin Evans.

The young outlaw did not look like a gunslinger when he reached Lincoln County. Apache Indians had stolen his horse, so he walked the last miles to a ranch house. The rancher's wife fed him and nursed his bloody feet. When the Kid left, she loaned him a horse.

The Kid was now calling himself Billy Bonney. He again joined up with Jesse Evans and his gang. In a short time the gang's thefts of livestock were the talk of Lincoln County. Sheriff Brady locked up Evans and three of his men. The "jail" was a hole in the ground topped with a log guardroom. Billy and the rest of the gang rescued their friends. Most of the outlaws fled, but the Kid stayed in the county.

Four hundred people lived in the town of Lincoln. It was the center of county life. A mile of mud-brick buildings lined a shady street. The town's only two-story building housed a general store. Another building served as courtroom and dance hall.

Jimmy Dolan, who owned the general store, controlled Lincoln County. Dolan and his friends made money any way they could. They bought stolen cattle from the Evans gang for $5 a head. Then they sold the cattle to army soldiers for $15 a head.

The town was growing. Men moved in who did not

Jimmy Dolan (standing) and Lawrence Murphy ruled Lincoln County in the 1870s. They were tough, ruthless men. Because Billy worked for their enemies, he became their enemy as well.

John Tunstall hired Billy to work on his ranch. He treated Billy fairly and became his friend. After Tunstall died at the hands of Jimmy Dolan's men, the Kid vowed revenge.

like Jimmy Dolan. A rancher named John Tunstall fought back. With the help of a lawyer named Alexander McSween, Tunstall opened a second general store in Lincoln. As Dolan's profits fell, he tried to scare Tunstall into leaving. Tunstall told his foreman to hire some gunmen.

Billy was hired to work on the Tunstall ranch. The rancher liked the Kid and treated him fairly. In return, Billy gave Tunstall his loyalty. If there was shooting, the Kid said he would fight for his new friend.

The Kid did not have long to wait. McSween had been hired to collect $47,000 for one of Dolan's friends. McSween did so, but held on to the money. Some of it was owed to him, and he claimed he was not sure who should get the rest. That was too much for Dolan's friend. He charged the lawyer with breaking the law. A judge signed an order that tied up all of McSween's money.

Dolan saw his chance. He was sure that McSween owned half of Tunstall's store. With Sheriff Brady's backing, Dolan took over the store. The loss of the store made Tunstall and McSween angry. The rancher told his men to ride with their guns loaded. The war was about to start.

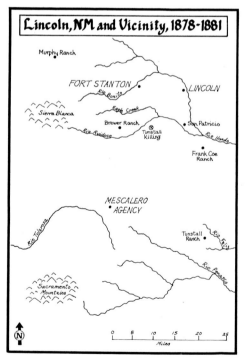

The Lincoln County war brought years of bloodshed to New Mexico. Many men died in the fight for control of Lincoln and the ranchland around it.

4

THE KID GOES TO WAR

A few days passed. The shooting started when Sheriff Brady sent a posse to the Tunstall ranch. Sheriff Brady had a legal paper that said some of the ranch's horses belonged to McSween. His men had orders to round up these horses for delivery to Dolan.

The posse met Tunstall, Billy, and three cowboys near the ranch. Billy and the cowboys took cover in some trees. Tunstall made the mistake of staying to talk. A deputy pulled a gun and killed him.

Now it was a real war. Dolan was backed by Sheriff Brady, the district judge, and the Evans gang. The town constable and the justice of the peace sided with McSween. Tunstall's men formed a posse of gunmen who also sided with McSween. Billy joined the Regulators, as Tunstall's men were called. He was eager to avenge Tunstall's death.

Most of Lincoln County hoped that McSween would defeat Dolan. Then two bloody events changed people's minds. First, the Regulators caught two men from the posse that killed Tunstall. The men gave up, thinking they would be taken back to town. But Billy and a friend killed both of them in cold blood.

Next, the Regulators plotted to kill Sheriff Brady. Billy and five others hid behind the general store one night. They opened fire when Sheriff Brady and two deputies left the courthouse the next morning. The shots killed Brady and one deputy. When Billy ran out to grab Brady's rifle, the second deputy shot him in the leg.

Lincoln looks peaceful enough in this picture. But men died on the town's main street during the Lincoln County war. Billy the Kid was mixed up in a number of the shootings.

Sheriff William Brady took Jimmy Dolan's side during the Lincoln County war. Billy was part of the gang that ambushed him. When Brady stepped out of the courthouse he was cut down by rifle fire.

Somehow, the Kid managed to drag himself to safety. His friends in town hid him while the wound healed.

A grand jury charged that both sides were to blame for the killings. The charges did not settle the feud. A new gunfight broke out in April. A troop of U.S. Army soldiers had to be called in to end the shooting.

The last battle began the night of June 14, 1878. McSween led sixty Regulators into Lincoln. They turned two stores and the McSween home into forts. The new sheriff and his posse dug in to face McSween and his men. For three days the two sides fired at anything that moved. But neither side would give up.

Word of the fighting reached the army. Soldiers led by Colonel Nathan Dudley moved in with heavy guns and cannons. It soon became clear that Colonel Dudley favored the Dolan side. He ordered the gunners to aim at McSween's makeshift forts. Many of the defenders fled when they saw the cannons.

McSween held out in his house, but the sheriff's men set it on fire. Choking in the smoke, Billy told those who were left to run for the river. Everyone escaped but McSween. His white shirt was an easy target. A burst of gunfire cut him down.

The Lincoln County war ended with McSween's death. Neither side could say it had won. Without a leader, many of the Regulators drifted away. For his part, Dolan was out of cash.

The Kid stayed in Lincoln to be near his friends. The gang of ex-Regulators kept things stirred up. They stole horses and made threats against Dolan. Following the Code of the West, they wanted revenge for the deaths of Tunstall and McSween.

In August 1878, Billy found some more trouble. He was riding with the gang near a trading post called the Mescalero Apache Agency. Billy and half of the gang stopped to drink at a spring. The others rode toward the post. All at once some Indians opened fire on them. Inside, the agency chief and his clerk heard the shots.

Susan McSween stood behind her husband during the Lincoln County war. Some say she played the piano while the two sides fired at each other. Later, she tried to take legal action against Jimmy Dolan.

The two men thought the gang was coming to kill them. They tried to flee, only to run into the angry gang members. Guns roared and the clerk fell dead. The agency chief retreated to the trading post.

Out at the spring, the gunfire spooked the Kid's horse. It ran off, leaving him on foot. Ducking as bullets zipped near his head, the Kid jumped onto George Coe's horse. With Billy riding double, George and the others circled the agency. Billy caught a pony in the agency's corral and rode it bareback to the gang's hideout.

News of the shootout spread quickly. Everyone blamed the Kid for the clerk's death. Colonel Dudley sent soldiers to arrest him. The soldiers came back

John Chisum was one of the richest ranchers of the Old West. He helped Tunstall and McSween in their battle against Jimmy Dolan. His niece Sallie was Billy's sweetheart for a while.

empty-handed. The Kid and his friends had already left the county.

A week later Billy turned up at the ranch of John Chisum. Chisum had been Tunstall's friend and owned a large ranch. Sallie Chisum, the owner's niece, was said to be one of the Kid's sweethearts. The Chisums were moving their herd north to Fort Sumner. Billy went with them.

The Kid spent his nights dancing with the girls of Fort Sumner. But he still wanted revenge for the events in Lincoln. He sent word for some of the old gang to join him.

In late September, the gang stole some horses. Then they drove them to Texas to sell. The ranchers there bought the horses, no questions asked. Billy stayed in Texas for a month. Then he headed back toward Lincoln. One by one his gang left him. Only his best friend, Tom O'Folliard, still rode with the Kid.

Somewhere on the trail Billy changed his mind. He was no longer thinking about revenge. He hoped to end his problems with the law. For once in his life, the Kid wanted to make peace.

Tom O'Folliard was one of Billy's closest friends. He stayed with Billy after many of the Kid's gang had fled to safety. Tom died in an ambush set up by Pat Garrett.

5

THE KID'S FAME GROWS

It was now 1879, one year after Tunstall's death. Billy said there had been enough shooting. Dolan's gunmen agreed to meet him in Lincoln for a talk.

Twenty men met in the middle of the street. Jesse Evans screamed that Billy could not be trusted. He said they should kill the Kid right there. Billy said he was not there to fight. His words calmed the hot tempers. Then the two sides agreed to end the killing. They also promised not to testify in court. If someone did, the others vowed to kill him. The terms were written down and they all signed the paper.

The two gangs went to a saloon, where Dolan joined them. Billy was one of the few who stayed sober. Later that night the drunken party met Huston Chapman in the street. Chapman was a lawyer who had been hired

For all his fame, only two pictures of Billy the Kid have been found. In this posed picture, the Kid faces the camera, guns close to hand.

to bring legal charges against McSween's killers. Dolan and his friends hated him.

A Dolan man named Bill Campbell pulled a pistol. He ordered Chapman to dance for him. The lawyer refused. All at once Dolan fired his pistol into the ground. Startled by the sound, Campbell pulled the trigger of his own gun. Chapman fell with a bullet in his chest. His killers left him there and went on to a second saloon.

Word of the murder brought New Mexico's governor to Lincoln. Lew Wallace had been a Civil War general. In later years he won fame as the author of *Ben Hur*. At this time, his job was to end the shooting. One step was to offer a pardon to those who had not been indicted by a grand jury. That did not help Billy. The Kid had already been indicted for two killings.

In March, Billy wrote to Governor Wallace to ask for a meeting. He said he would testify in court about the Chapman murder. This broke his promise to Dolan and his men. But the Kid badly wanted a pardon. Wallace agreed to meet with him.

Billy gave himself up a week later. Wallace placed the Kid under guard in the house next door to his own. Billy met with the governor and told him about his life as an outlaw. Wallace then went back to Santa Fe without giving Billy a pardon.

The grand jury met in April. Many of its members were McSween's friends. Billy named Dolan and Campbell as Chapman's killers. The jury, in turn, indicted the two men for murder. It also indicted Colonel Dudley for burning the McSween house.

The Kid stayed to serve as a witness, but Campbell fled the county. When the trials were held, the juries refused to convict Dolan. Then the district attorney pulled a double cross. He filed papers to put Billy on trial. The Kid was charged with the murder of Sheriff Brady.

Because he was still hoping for a pardon, Billy felt betrayed. He climbed on his horse and rode out of Lincoln. Some people said the new sheriff looked the other way. If so, he must have agreed that Billy had been treated badly.

The Kid went to Fort Sumner. The small town was a hundred miles northeast of Lincoln. Although he was a wanted man, Billy was welcome there. Mexican sheep-herders gave him a place to sleep. Some of the local girls fell in love with his boyish good looks. Billy dealt cards in the saloons to keep busy. He also had a good time at the town's weekly dances.

Fort Sumner was a meeting place for outlaws that summer. Some had been driven west by the Texas state police. Others came in on the Santa Fe railroad. Some of the old gang members teamed up with Billy. Together they stole horses and cattle.

The Kid added to his legend that summer. A cowboy named Joe Grant had been bragging that he was going

These are two of the most famous guns in American history. These deadly colts helped Billy the Kid become one of the West's most famous gunslingers. The best guess is that Billy killed nine men—not twenty-one.

Billy the Kid

41 Caliber Double Action Colt Revolver. Billy the Kid used this gun as a holster weapon. He favored the small curved grip on this type gun because his hands were small and they fitted him better. The kid painted a very sordid picture in the short time he lived in the Southwest. There was nothing brave or romantic in it. He would just as soon shoot a man in the back as face him.

Billy the Kid

41 Caliber Colt Double Action Revolver. This was Colt's first double action gun and with this short barrel it made a satisfactory pocket weapon. Billy was supposed to have killed 21 men before he was 21 years old. He was finally killed by Sheriff Pat Garrett in New Mexico.

to kill the Kid. Grant was drunk when he followed Billy into a saloon one night. Billy had to think fast. He pulled Grant's gun from its holster, saying he liked its looks. Quickly, he turned the cylinder. Then Billy gave the gun back. Now the hammer would fall on an empty chamber if Grant pulled the trigger.

Grant tried hard to start a fight. He yelled that he was going to shoot one of Billy's friends. Billy told him he was aiming at the wrong man. Grant called Billy a liar. Billy shrugged and walked away. Grant aimed his pistol at Billy's back and pulled the trigger. The hammer clicked on the empty chamber. When he heard the click, Billy drew his gun. Spinning around, he killed Grant with three quick shots.

Not long after that, Billy went to see John Chisum. Billy said that Chisum had not paid him for his work in Lincoln County. Chisum laughed and told Billy he had been paid fairly. Billy was angry, but he did not want to kill the old man. With the help of his gang he stole some of Chisum's cattle instead.

Almost every rancher was losing cattle to rustlers. They wanted a strong sheriff who could protect their herds. John Chisum's choice was a six-foot six-inch man named Pat Garrett. Garrett was new to the job but he was honest, smart, and tough. The former bartender also knew Billy's hiding places. At first, Garrett served as a deputy sheriff. In fact, he was not given his badge as county sheriff until January 1, 1881.

The Kid's fame as a gunslinger was growing. If a crime took place in New Mexico, Billy was said to be behind it. One story said he was passing fake money. Other men swore that he was robbing the U.S. mails. Billy's gang did steal sixteen horses. A posse trailed the outlaws to a house near White Oaks, New Mexico. One of the posse named Jimmy Carlyle went inside to talk the gang into giving up. Someone in the house pulled a gun and killed the unarmed Carlyle. After a long stand-off the posse gave up and rode off. The Kid was free to lead his gang away into the night.

The press wrote that "Billy the Kid" had shot Carlyle. It was the first time this nickname was seen in print. Governor Wallace was angered by the killing. He put up a large reward for Billy's capture.

Sheriff Pat Garrett (left) posing with two deputies, was tall, tough, and quick on the trigger. The Kid escaped from jail the first time Garrett caught him. The next time they met, the sheriff shot first and asked questions later.

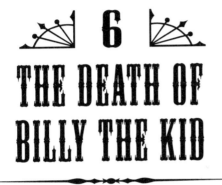

6
THE DEATH OF BILLY THE KID

The Kid returned to Fort Sumner as winter closed in. He visited friends, went to dances, and slept in an old building.

Garrett heard that the Kid was in town. The deputy sheriff saw a chance to catch the young outlaw. He reached Fort Sumner on December 17, 1880. But Billy was gone when he got there.

The Kid and his gang came back during a snow storm. Perhaps Billy sensed that Garrett and his posse were waiting. At the last minute he moved to the rear of the line of riders. The posse opened fire as the outlaws rode into the trap. Tom O'Folliard was killed, but Billy and the others escaped.

The posse tracked the outlaws to a stone hut near Stinking Springs. At first light Garrett saw another of Billy's gang standing in the doorway. Rifles cracked. The man fell back into the tiny hut. He staggered out a minute later, his hands in the air. The wounds were fatal, and he died within the hour.

Billy's only hope was to escape on horseback. He tried to pull a horse into the hut but Garrett shot it. The dead horse now blocked the only way out. Garrett called to Billy to give up. Billy yelled back, "Come and get me."

Those words sounded tough, but the men in the hut were out of food. The smell of the posse's cooking fires made their mouths water. Soon Billy and the others came out with their hands up.

Garrett took his captives to a jail in Las Vegas, New Mexico. Billy was cheerful enough. He talked with a reporter while he tried on a new suit, a gift from a friend. The Kid liked the suit, but thought the jail was terrible. "Is the jail at Santa Fe any better than this?" he asked.

Billy was moved to the Santa Fe jail and spent the next three months there. He wrote to Governor Wallace to ask about the pardon he had been promised. Wallace did not reply. In March, the Kid was sent to Mesilla, New Mexico and put on trial. The trial lasted just one day. On April 13, 1881, the Kid was sentenced to be hanged.

Garrett moved Billy to the Lincoln County court-house. To prevent an escape attempt, he chained the Kid with handcuffs and leg irons. Two men, Bob Olinger and James Bell, were ordered to guard the prisoner. Olinger was a cruel man. He insulted Billy and hit him when no one else was around.

Judge Warren Bristol was an old friend of Jimmy Dolan. When he tried Billy for murder, the judge quickly sentenced Billy to be hung. Billy could have asked for a new trial, but he could not pay the court fees.

The Kid's chance to escape came on April 28. Garrett left to buy lumber for the scaffold on which Billy would be hanged. Olinger was away from the jail. The Kid asked Bell to take him to the outdoor toilet. He found a gun there, hidden by a friend. On the way back Billy slipped one wrist out of the handcuffs. Bell tried to run, but he was not quick enough. Billy shot him in the back. Then the Kid picked up a shotgun. He killed Olinger when the guard came back to the courthouse.

Next, Billy used a pickax to break one of the leg irons. With the chain tucked into his belt, he climbed on a horse and rode away. No one tried to stop him.

The Kid did not go far after he left Lincoln. He rode to a nearby house where a friend cut off his chains.

Another friend gave Billy a horse. The man urged him to flee to Mexico. Billy shook his head. He said he would go back to Fort Sumner instead.

Nine days later Billy reached Fort Sumner. This time he was more careful. He slept at farms and sheep camps. At night he liked to sneak into Fort Sumner to go to dances. On other nights he went to see his sweethearts.

In May, the Las Vegas paper wrote that Billy was at Fort Sumner. The news amazed Sheriff Garrett. He thought Billy would be far away by now. Three months after Billy's escape Garret saddled up a three-man posse.

Garrett and his men reached Fort Sumner on July 14, 1881. They stayed out of sight because Billy had friends there. That night the lawmen set up a trap. With luck,

The Lincoln County Courthouse had once been a general store. The Kid was due to be hung when he broke out of jail here. During his escape Billy gunned down two guards. He was standing on the balcony when he shot Bob Olinger. After that no one tried to stop him when he rode out of town.

Bob Olinger was one of Billy's guards at the Lincoln County Court-house. Olinger took pleasure in teasing and punching Billy. He paid for his cruelty with his life.

the Kid would walk right into it. But no one saw him slip into Celsa Gutiérrez's house. Celsa was one of his sweethearts.

The lawmen talked it over. Were they wasting their time? Garrett said he would talk to Pete Maxwell, an old friend who might be able to tell them where Billy was.

His men stayed outside while he went into Maxwell's bedroom. It was near midnight when he sat down on the older man's bed.

Back at Celsa's house Billy said he was hungry. He knew that Pete Maxwell had a side of meat hanging on his porch. Still in his stocking feet, he headed for Maxwell's house. Knife in hand, he was ready to carve himself a steak.

Billy almost bumped into Garrett's men. Springing back, he drew his pistol. In a whisper he said, "*¿Quién es?*"—Spanish for "Who are you?" The men did not

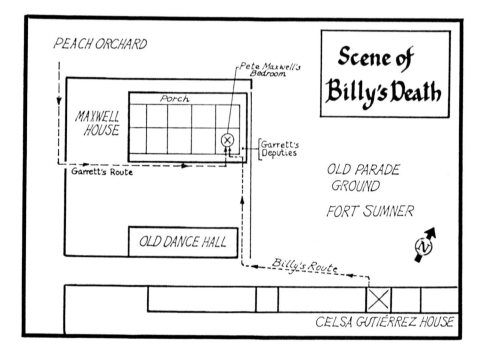

This map shows the paths taken by Pat Garrett and Billy the night of July 14, 1881. The Kid's luck ran out when he went to the Maxwell house to find a snack.

Billy the Kid died in a downstairs bedroom of this house. Surprised to find two strangers on the porch, Billy ran into Pete Maxwell's bedroom. Pat Garrett was already there, his gun close at hand.

know the stranger was Billy the Kid. One of the men told him not to be afraid.

By now Maxwell was awake. He told Garrett that Billy was staying at a sheep ranch near town. Then the two men heard the voices outside. A moment later someone entered the darkened room.

"Who are those fellows outside, Pete?" a voice asked.

Maxwell sat up and yelled, "That's him!"

Billy now saw the figure sitting next to Maxwell.

"*¿Quién es? ¿Quién es?*" he demanded.

Garrett also knew the voice. He drew his pistol and fired twice. Billy fell dead with a bullet near his heart.

The shots brought people running from nearby houses. Some of the men and women cursed Garrett for killing the Kid. The sheriff and his men had to stay on guard all night. They feared that Billy's friends would attack them.

A jury ruled that Garrett shot the Kid in the line of duty. On July 15, 1881, Billy the Kid was buried at Fort Sumner. The young gunslinger was only 21 years old.

Billy the Kid might have lived longer had he left New Mexico. But he chose to stay in Fort Sumner. Now he lies close to two pals beneath this tombstone.

7
THE LEGEND OF BILLY THE KID

Why is Billy the Kid so well-known? Unlike Jesse James, Billy never robbed a bank. He never held up a train or blew up a safe. The gangs he ran with never made much money from their crimes. In fact, his life as an outlaw lasted only four years.

It is true that Billy was quick on the trigger. A good guess is that he killed nine men. That was not even close to a record for those violent times. John Wesley Hardin, a less well-known gunslinger, killed forty-four men.

The Billy the Kid most people think they know is a legend. The legend says that Billy killed his first man to protect his mother's name. After that he spent his short life fighting bad men like Jimmy Dolan. In this romantic legend, the Kid kills a man for each of his twenty-one years. He becomes a western Robin Hood. Why did he steal? Why, to help the poor, of course.

THE FIVE CENT
WIDE AWAKE
LIBRARY

Entered according to Act of Congress, in the year 1881, by FRANK TOUSEY, in the office of the Librarian of Congress, at Washington, D. C.

Entered at the Post Office at New York, N. Y., as Second Class Matter.

No. 451. | COMPLETE. | FRANK TOUSEY, PUBLISHER, 20 ROSE STREET, N. Y. NEW YORK, August 29, 1881. | ISSUED EVERY MONDAY. | PRICE 5 CENTS. | Vol. I.

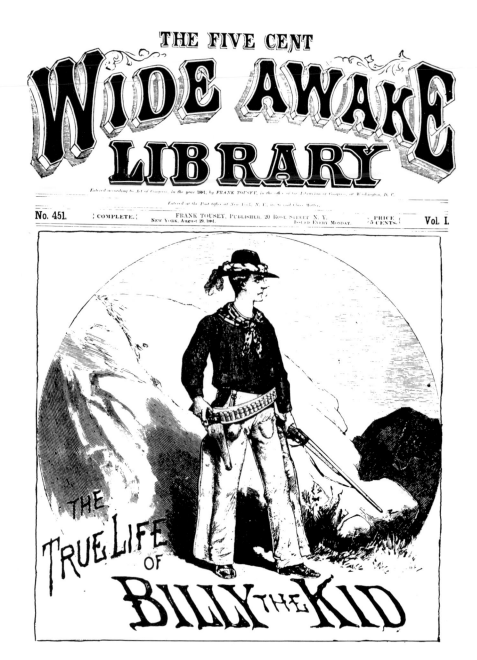

THE TRUE LIFE OF BILLY THE KID

Dime novels were quick to cash in on Billy's fame. The Wide Awake Library's readers did not know that Billy looked nothing like this drawing. Nor did they care that the magazine's "true life" story was more fiction than fact. All they wanted was an exciting story.

How did such a legend get started? It began with stories told about Billy while he was alive. After Billy's death, Pat Garrett "wrote" *The Authentic Life of Billy the Kid.* The book's real author was Ash Upson, a New Mexico postmaster. Upson made up many of the stories in the book.

Next, many dime novels borrowed freely from the Garrett-Upson book. After the dime novels came the movies. Most films picture Billy as an outlaw-hero. This Billy came to life again in the 1988 movie, *Young Guns.* This was followed in 1990 by *Young Guns II.*

Writers will always argue over the facts of the Kid's life. Only one truth is certain. The legend of Billy the Kid will never die.

Ash Upson played a big role in creating the legend of Billy the Kid. Upson was the "ghost" who really wrote Pat Garrett's book about Billy. For many years most people thought the stories Upson made up were true.

GLOSSARY

Apache Agency—A trading post for Indians sponsored by the U.S. government.

avenge—To get even with someone for a wrongdoing.

boarder—Someone who pays for a room and meals in a home.

Code of the West—The unwritten rules men and women tried to live by in the Wild West.

constable—A law officer who keeps the peace in a town or village.

dime novels—Low-cost magazines that printed popular fiction during the late 1800s.

famine—A time when food is scarce and people starve.

foreman—The person in charge of a work crew.

grand jury—A jury that has the job of deciding whether or not a suspect should stand trial for a crime.

gunslinger—Outlaws and lawmen of the Wild West who settled arguments with their guns.

indicted—To be charged with a crime.

jury—A group of people sworn to judge the facts and make a decision on a given matter.

justice of the peace (JP) —A lower court official who hears minor cases. JPs also have the power to marry people and to send cases to the higher courts.

legend—A story that many people believe but which is almost always untrue.

pardon—A legal document that forgives someone for any crimes he or she may have committed.

posse—A group of citizens who join with law enforcement officers to aid in the capture of outlaws.

Regulators—The name given to the gunslingers who supported Tunstall and McSween in the Lincoln County war.

rustler—Someone who steals horses or cattle.

scaffold—The platform on which a convicted criminal is hanged.

sombrero—A Spanish name for a wide-brimmed hat often worn in the Southwest and in Mexico.

MORE GOOD READING
ABOUT BILLY THE KID

Breihan, Carl W. with Marion Ballert. *Billy the Kid: A Date With Destiny*. Superior, Wis.: Superior Publishing Co., 1970.

Garrett, Pat F. *The Authentic Life of Billy the Kid*. Norman, Okla.: University of Oklahoma Press, 1954.

Horan, James D. "Billy the Kid," in *The Authentic Wild West: the Gunfighters*. New York: Crown Publishers, 1976, pp. 9–80.

Lyon, Peter. "Billy the Kid," in *The Wild, Wild West*. Ramsey, N.J.: Funk & Wagnalls, 1969, pp. 117–124.

Trachtman, Paul, and editors of Time-Life Books. "Sinister Masters of Murder," in *The Gunfighters*. Alexandria, Va.: Time-Life Books, 1974, pp. 166–193.

Utley, Robert M. *Billy the Kid. A Short and Violent Life*. Lincoln, Nebr.: University of Nebraska Press, 1989.

INDEX

47